VOICE

Poetry by the Youth of Kalihi

Students of Farrington High School
Author

Cover designed by Calvin Bagaoisan

Printed in the United States of America

First Printing: April 2019
W. R. Farrington High School
www.farringtonhighschool.org
voice@farringtonhighschool.org

ISBN-13: 978-1-0929-9647-1
Imprint: Independently published

"In a lot of societies, art and poetry is considered to be a garnish—something pretty to add on to something—and that's just not true. It has the capacity to heal..."
- *Kathy Jetnil-Kijiner*

These poems are

For our parents, our family, our friends,
For teenagers, couples, and those who fall in love.
For the islands of Micronesia.
For all people.
And for ourselves.

For our parents, our family, our friends,
For tradition and for our future.
For Farrington High School,
For Simmi and all the islands of Chuuk.
For our generation and people who share our feelings,
For all Chuukese people.
And for ourselves.

For our family and friends,
For our sisters and brothers.
For the people in Hawai'i.
For all students.
For our dreams.
And for ourselves.

For all families who care for their children,
For people who struggle with social structures,
And for Poseidon.

Para sa mga tawo nga palangga ko
For the people I love,
Dagiti naibatik nga ay-ayatek
For the loved ones I left behind,
Ti marikriknak kenni nanangko
For what I feel for my mom,
Ken para ti bagik
And for myself.

For myself,
For my caring mom,
For mom and dad,
For my lola,
For my uncle,
And for my haters.

For those who are about to give up,
And for the troubled youth.

CONTENTS

Foreword 1

Letter to the Poets 3

Change.. 5

Family 21

Healing 37

Home... 53

Poets 65

Teachers 121

Mahalo... 126

FOREWORD

We spend our days with culturally and linguistically diverse students who are all part of the English Language Learner (ELL) program at Farrington High School. Every day our students inspire us, make us laugh, stress us out, but most of all, they make us talk. Through our endless conversations, we noticed that across all of our classes students believed that they do not have a voice, despite the wide variety of experiences and perspectives they bring to our school.

In one of our classes, we asked them to stand in a circle and to move to the center when they heard a statement that related to them. Everyone, including us, moved to the center when we stated, "I was born outside of Hawai'i." Unsurprisingly, all of us also moved to the center when we stated, "I speak and understand more than one language." But when we called, "I have a voice," the majority of students did not attempt to move and some were unsure. When asked why this was, one of them confessed, "We are just students," which is synonymous with: we are just immigrants; we are just from Kalihi; we are just ELLs; we do not matter.

This left us with a teachable moment not only for our students, but also for ourselves. This project was intended to create a platform for the voices of these often underrepresented and unheard students. They carry with them stories of immigration, separation from family, changing homes, searching for identity, and what it means to be an adolescent in today's Hawai'i.

As we worked towards empowering our students, we partnered with Asian American and Pacific Islander (AAPI) authors and community organizations who ushered them into the growing world of AAPI literature. Our students were mentored by poets and authors, many of whom share the same student experiences of immigrating to the United States, growing up in an immigrant family, and learning English as a second, third, or even fourth language. Care was taken to keep the authenticity of students' poetic voice and students were

1

encouraged to express themselves not only in English, but also in the language or dialect they felt was best.

In this anthology, you will find poems sharing the experiences our students wish others knew about them. You will find poems written by students born in Hawaiʻi while living in multilingual families and who are navigating the disconnect between living in two conflicting cultures. You will find poems written by newcomer students who are adjusting to a new culture, a new school, and a new home. You will also find poems written by 1.5 generation immigrant students who continually grapple with what it means to fit into mainstream American culture while keeping hold of the traditions and values they carried with them into this country.

We hope this anthology amplifies our students' voices as they heal from their experiences, celebrate their stories, and navigate their journeys. We wish to extend this conversation of student voice and experience outside of our classrooms and into schools and homes across the nation. We hope you are able to learn as much from our students as we learn from them every day.

Thank you for listening to their stories.

Elianna Kantar
Norman Sales
Akiko Giambelluca
Rachel Jun

LETTER TO THE POETS

April 15, 2019

Dear Poets,

A deep heartfelt thank you for sharing your stories of joy, struggles, resistance, perseverance, and gratitude with the world. Your multilingual poems resonated with me and triggered memories of my own upbringing and experiences. And they also gave me a peek into the lives of our different languages and cultures in Hawaiʻi.

Like many of you, I didn't want to be "me" when I was growing up. I faced prejudice and discrimination and was ashamed of being Filipino. I was ashamed of my parents' accents. I was ashamed of speaking Tagalog. And up until this day, I regret not maintaining my home language. However, like many of you, my family and culture were the source of grounding and strength. I treasure the values and traditions of my family and community.

As I grew older, I converted my shame into a mission to make sure no child would ever experience what I did growing up. That's why I became a teacher. So when my Cambodian 1st grade student Chenda wanted to change her name to Linda to make it easier for others to pronounce, I convinced her to keep her unique name. When I pursued graduate school, I studied multicultural education. And when I became a member of the Hawaiʻi State Board of Education, I spearheaded the Seal of Biliteracy and other multilingual policies and practices to promote our languages and cultures as imperative to our academic success.

You are fortunate to have teachers who create an educational environment that uplift your voices. Embrace where you are from and your lived experiences. Stand up and be heard because you have a story to tell. And use your voice passionately and wisely to make the world a better place.

Aloha,

Patricia Halagao, PhD
Professor, University of Hawaiʻi at Mānoa
Former Member, Hawaiʻi State Board of Education (2013-2016)

CHANGE

Poetry by the Youth of Kalihi

Be Good to Yourself
John John Daluping

Just because I am Filipino,
Doesn't mean I am rude
Doesn't mean I am dull
I am a helpful boy.
I go with my father to take out trash
I assist my mother to clean the house.

Just because I am small,
Doesn't mean I am weak
Doesn't mean I am bad at volleyball
Doesn't mean I cannot reach my goal
I am a determined person.
I study hard
I want to become a fireman
so I can make my parents smile.

Just because I am skinny,
Doesn't mean I do not eat well
Doesn't mean I am not strong inside
Doesn't mean I am slow.
I run fast and nobody can catch me
I always run for fun with my friends
I want to become a professional runner.

Don't Judge by My Cover
AJ Peralta

Just because I'm Filipino
Doesn't mean I'm silly
I listen carefully to the teachers and my parents
    Doesn't mean I'm stupid
        I work hard, acting like a high schooler
        with critical thinking skills
    Doesn't mean I can't speak English
      I have many local friends
      I can communicate in English
        I'm a good person

Just because I'm a boy
    Doesn't mean I don't cry
      I cry when my feet and my arm broke
      And it's okay to show my emotion
    Doesn't mean I'm rude
      I'm not like other men who do not respect women
    Doesn't mean I can't hang out with girls
      I can choose who I hang out with
      and it doesn't mean I'm gay
        I'm a polite person

Dream is the thing with wings
Hanting Zhou

Dream is the thing with wings
That soars in the sky
Like blooming flowers
Trying to go high
Plant them in my heart
To take root and germinate

Seize the opportunities
Dreams haunt you like elves
It touches you when you never give up
It must be soft
It exudes a scent when you never lose hope
It must be sweet

Tick tock
Tick tock
When dreams fly in, warm,
The sun shines all over the room

FAITH *(Nùkùnùk)*

Trinity Stephen

Finding the steps that lead to my dream.
Kutta mesen ipwei epwe emweni ei ngeni ai we áneán.

Always reaching higher.
Achocho ngeni met mei nomw pekilon fansoun meinisin.

Into the darkness.
Non kiroch.

Touching the clouds, smooth and fresh.
Attapa kuchu mi motoutou me séfé.

Hoping to feel the rough edges of a dream still unknown.
Anean upwe mefi tárupwun nesopun ai onottan ika mwo ese mwo fen fatèoch ngeni ei.

Good Student, Strong Daughter

Jonalyn Daluping

Just because I am Filipino
Doesn't mean I am poor
Doesn't mean I am not good at speaking English
Doesn't mean I am a small person
I am a good student
Listening to my teacher and
Doing my best to meet deadlines

Just because I am a girl
Doesn't mean I am weak
Doesn't mean I am disgusting
Doesn't mean I am lazy
I am a strong daughter and reliable sister
Cleaning the house, washing the clothes,
Taking care of my brother
Though I am younger than him

Just because I am an ELL student
Doesn't mean I am stupid
Doesn't mean I am uncool
Doesn't mean I am naughty
I am a diligent student
Keeping up with my homework
Dreaming about going to college

HIGH SCHOOL IS A GAME

Adrian James F. Lo

In high school our reputation is held on a rope
One mistake and the rumor is spread.
You need to keep your head high
Just pass by and ignore hurtful words
But protect the people in need.

Top dogs have a bark that can scare you away
And the underdogs that follow them too.
But have no fear it's just part of the game
That everyone plays.
Nobody said the game was easy
It can be hard and confusing.
But the struggle you face will build
The person you are.

Your abilities can take you to the top
So when the day comes
Take the stage, hold the diploma
Get the prize for playing well.

I am a va'a

Tuieteuati Alai

I came from a very small village called Aua in American Samoa
I moved to Kalihi to pursue my education
Have a great life and focus in school
So that I could achieve my goals:
Pursue a college degree, buy whatever
my parents want, become an actor

In American Samoa, in the past, there were two giants
lua lapoa who are brothers, uso
Their names were Matafao and Pioa
but they always argued
Later on, Matafao and Pioa passed away
on the same day
and became the two biggest mountains in American Samoa

They are the most important mountains of all time
because they're big, tall, and beautiful
like my parents who always fight when it comes down
to financial and family issues
I am a va'a who is still rowing to find answers
to help my parents

Samoans are known as happy people
Because everyone knows the culture
That is God first, Family second, and last is your Future
We are small but a unique island

Jojo To Friend
Wojila Chutaro

Well, friend I'll tell you:
Love for me ain't no joke.
It has fire
It's hot

Sometimes I cry from it
Nowhere and nothing can solve it
So, when I say I love you
Please believe it's true.

Tõmak im kõjatdrikdrik

When I say forever
Know I'll never leave you.
So don't turn back
'Cause if you stop now it can burn us.

When the darkness looks dangerous
Remember I'll always be there,
To brighten your day.

Keemejmej bwe Iroij ej meram eo.

I know it's hard but keep goin'

'Cause love for me
Ain't no joke.

Kwek-Kwek
Christian Cobrador

I am standing in front of my class
With my fellow students staring at me
With my teacher listening to me
With everyone's attention on me

Tell them I came to Hawai'i on June 7, 2018
Tell them how amazed I was with the beauty of Hawai'i
Tell them of the similarities with Negros Occidental
The weather, crops, food, and the people

Also tell them how bored I was in Hawai'i
The longing that I've had
for my family and friends left in the Philippines
Tell them about the sweet taste of kwek-kwek
A boiled egg covered with red dough
that we usually eat with our cousins
Tell them I was a dying rose back in Manila
waiting for my plane to depart
Tell them how hard it felt without proper goodbyes
Without seeing the people I want to see

Tell them it's hard to be an immigrant

Tell them
Tell them...

Me to My Friend
Chan Ai Nguyen

Well, friend, I'll tell you
Every day for me has never been easy
Always challenging
If I draw my days on the map,
Every moment is a deep hole.

Trick me and bury me
But after all
I'm still here and if someone asks me
"You'll choose pass or stay there?"
My answer is always "pass"
Though hard problems push me back.

When everything goes to the dead end
My sky without any light
Even when I have cried many times
I told myself, keep tryin' to get out.

So friend don't give up, do not stop until successful.
There's no one behind you
Absolutely do not fall where you just stood up
When the waves of challenge come
As the sun rises and sun sets, difficulties will be solved.

Believe in yourself that you can handle it.
I'm still trying to make every day better,
As I said, every day for me has never been easy.

MyMy 2 Mom
Wersi Farata

Well Mom, i'll tell you
My life is a dream.

Like a tiger,
sweet but dangerous
waking up from her deep sleep
getting ready to do what she has to get done.

Beeping, slow breathing
Waves of worries
Heartbreaking river of tears
it's all up to me.

My dream trees are purple
And stars take away the night
The moaning moon lights up the sky
with me feeling dreams can be bright.

"Pumanawakon, agsubliakto"
Jalen Jor Espejo

I came to Hawai'i with happiness and sorrow in my pockets
With a smile on my face but cold droplets of tears in my eyes
Kasla bagyo a sumirsirip sadiay tangatang
Like a storm picking through the horizon

Leaving the place I call home to experience life in Paradise
Leaving friends and families behind

With their hands waving up high, saying their goodbyes
While I am tramping through a door
     Leading
          to
               a
                    brand new beginning
     Leading
        me
          to
             who knows where

Leaving memories
Saying, "*pumanawakon, agsubliakto*"

Sister to Brother
Lemin Xu

Well, Brother, I'll tell you
Life for me is an invisible prison.

Parents don't let me go out with my friends
So I don't have many friends.

My family does not believe me at all
I don't know what I did wrong.

I can only stay with you at home now,
I can only follow them now,
I cannot do anything I like.

So boy, do not turn back, grow up happily,
Do not be tied up like me,
Do what you love.

It's good for you to make more friends.
Learn more skills, you will be more free than me.

So that life for you is not a prison.
Be free.

The Boy Full of Desires
Ronilo A. Santander

Just because I am poor
Doesn't mean I cannot continue my education
Doesn't mean I cannot go to college
Doesn't mean I cannot pursue my goals in life
I am immovable
I want my parents to be proud of me

Just because I am not doing good at school
Doesn't mean I am not smart
Doesn't mean I am a bad student
Doesn't mean I am not learning anything
I am full of big dreams

I want to be a businessman,
get married,
And support my people

Just because I am Filipino
Doesn't mean I am stupid
Doesn't mean I cannot communicate with other people
Doesn't mean I cannot learn other languages
I am confident
I believe in myself, I am talented
I can sing and dance, I can make people happy

Turbulence

John Rosete

Well, I'll tell you this –
Life for me
is not a smooth flight

It has turbulence
It can burn to the ground
Large birds can get clipped on the engine
But there's always an emergency exit

And if I'm full of fuel
I can travel far
Where I belong,

The place that I've earned to rest,
With yellow soft sand and fresh coconuts
The isolation full of
LIFE

FAMILY

Poetry by the Youth of Kalihi

Brothers and Sisters Forever
Anisa Chikuo

I am from Nepanonong,
small and beautiful.
From eight brothers
From five sisters
Black hair, brown skin,
From Simion and Saimon.

I'm from island
Polle Neirenom.
Yummy rice and sweet breadfruit.
Missing my oldest brother Aster who is home in Chuuk
Feeling so sad like people crying at their funeral.

From sisters helping
each other clean house,
Brothers helping
each other cook dinners.
From sisters and brothers
praying together at church,
Brothers and sisters
talking stories.

Ngang seni Nepanonong, kúkkún me ningèoch.
Seni wanumèn mwáánii
Nimmèn pwii.
Seni mokùr mei chon, inis meii ènùkùng.
Seni Simion me Saimon.

Ngang seni Polle Neirenömw.
Rice mei annè me kön mei ar.
Uu pwositi mwáánii we wate Aster e nomw Chuuk.
Ai mefi riaffou me kechiw a ussun an aramas kechiw won mei
pe.

Seni pwii kewe rekan áninnis fengengen me nimeti non iimw,
Mwáánii kewe rekan áninnis fengen me kuk mwèngèn
nekkuniön.
Seni pwii me mwáánii kewe achocho iotek fengen non fáán.
Mwáánii me pwii akkasos fenge

Do you remember, Uncle
MJ Fuerte

When I was in the Philippines,
you always told us a joke
and made us laugh.

When you always picked us up
from the airport,
driving from Vigan to Manila.

At the kubo
we made fun of my friends
while they were sleeping.
We drew dots on their faces
making them look funny
with a black marker.

When we went to Paoay Sand Dunes
sand boarding and riding a truck.

I remember all of these
because you are one of the best Uncles
and I will never forget.

I do miss you
and more memories to come.

Family Love
Charleen Eram

I'm from Tol,
cooked breadfruit
and sweet rice,
I am from sunflowers,
nice and beautiful,
From parents,
loud and funny,
From Mackrity
and Mackrovii.
I'm from thousands of jokes
and laughing together
From talking about how
to respect people
and not fight
From the time my
mother left
Feeling sad like rainy days,
missing her like crazy
In storage,
clothes and pictures,
Memories of my grandpa.

Ngang seni Tol,
Echepw mei kuk
me rice mei arr,
Ngang seni sunflower,
ningèoch pwan katakat
Seni iin me saam,
osomwmwöng pwan atakirikir.
Seni Mackrity
me Mackrovii
Ngang seni ngèrèùn tàinikich
me atakirir fengen
Seni kapasen èùrèùren manawen
sùfènùti aramas
me kosapw fiu
Seni ewe otun inei we a no seniei
Uwa mefi weires ussun
pùngùngawen en ráán, poisiti
ussun upwe uwes.
Nön ewe soko, pisekii me nei
kewe sasing.
Achechemen semei we chinap.

Family Forever

Bermackson Ress

I am from an island,
small and beautiful,
also dangerous.
From humble and kind.
From Kathy and Mackress
I'm from the family that
knows respect
but also has a hard time
getting along
From believing in myself and
being generous to others.
I'm from the island of Pawnai.
Sweet breadfruit
Sticky rice, sweet fish
From the time
I fell off the boat
Sinking like someone was
pushing me down.
In my grandpa's room,
piano, ukulele.

Ngang seni ew fonu mi mwokkun
ningeoch nge fen
pwan onuokus.
Seni tipetekison me aramaseoch.
Seni Kathy me Mackress.
Ngang seni ew family mei sine
seufon
Nge mei pwan wor fansoun
tipefesen
Seni epinukunuk non ai tongeni
me fangafangeoch
Fngeni ekkoch aramas.
Ngang atin ewe fonu Pawnai.
Ammètun kön
Rice mi pachang, iik mi kapwich
Seni ewe fansoun u turutiw me
won ewe mota,
Tonong non sokkopaten osukosuk
Ai family chon anisiei
Ai family mei chok nonnomw rei

25

From Where
Dayson Berdon

I am from the oceanside, beautiful waves,
From many cousins and long black hair.
From Donby and Didi.
I'm from laughing together.
And praying before bed.
I'm from Udot, "Warriors pouding breadfruits on the clouds."
From my sister making up stories,
"The boy in the store asked, where is the mother of the eggs?"
In my suitcase, a photo of my Grandmother
Loving memories before she passed away.

Ngang atin Chuuk únúkún ewe saat mi niéoch
Mi chomong aramasem mi pwan enu–chonochon, tam mekurem.
Seni Donby me Didi.
Tatakir me pwapwa fengen.
Iotek mwemwen aipwene anut.
Ngang seni Udot, "ekewe chon nomw ir re nó pwo kón fan kuchu"
Fefinei we amen sine tútúnap. Usun an tútúnapei emon énuwén e nó
kamé ochan chukó non sitowa nge ese sinei iten chukó non merika
iwe a chok eisini ewe chón angang "ia upwe kuna me ian inen enan
sokun?"
Mi wor echo sasingin inei we chinap ee nóm non aiwe kiwifer
Achecheman mwemwen an ewe epwene sóponó.

Growing up in a poor family
Eddie Casallo

I came from a poor family
Who grew crops and other things
We made money but it wasn't enough

I was just a kid growing up like a crop
So much grass and corn around me
There's no place like any other
Than living in a country that looks like a jungle

But sometimes I call myself a mouse
Moves a lot and just stay in the house
Other people see me as a jumping boy

A kid who would always go school
Rather than being a plant staying in the dirt
Once I'm home I just stand there like corn
That my mom always prepared for me
Tasting like popcorn, sweet, easy to bite

But I feel that I'm just a kid
Growing up in a farm family
That treated me like a plant
Chilling by the indayon
Relaxed like corn in a windy field

Happiness in Me
Alodia Villanueva

My mom and I
cooked delicious pinakbet
when I was a child
In the village of Brgy. Cali
close to a green mountain
teaching me the family recipe
she learned from her mother

My sister and I
dancing budots while singing
whenever we feel like it
In our bathroom playing soap bubbles
while scrubbing the white dull tub
that makes cleaning fun and joyful together

My family and I
invite more than ten relatives and friends
to our picnic during the winter break
right before school starts
at Ala Moana Beach
speaking Ilokano loudly
sharing pinakbet and pancit
enjoying every passing moment

KAZOKU

Maremingy Alifios

Spending happy times with family
Smiles appear on their faces
enjoying these moments
I realize joy in me races

Tears of satisfaction fall down my cheek
Hearing the sweetest words I. Love. You.
Love is a strong feeling and it is true
But my family's love is what I seek

Like some families, my family also has problems
Arguing and complaining about our education
But through the problems, there is always a solution
I'm the one that always has a conclusion

Me and My Brother
James Zyrus Comision

Me and my brother
Going to a big mall, Gaisano in Cagayan de Oro
Sweet smell of Kaldereta
Havana playing as the background music
Many people buying shoes or clothes
Irving shoes, his favorite shoes
For his 6th birthday.

Me and my brother
Vacationing in my father's town, Bukidnon Dangcagan
Beautiful place with rows and rows of rice fields,
Green and yellow.
I heard mooing, neighing, oinking, and chirping
For vacation to visit my cousins
Because my brother and I missed them

Me and my brother, Mark.
I miss his high, loud, but sweet voice
Calling me "Kuya"
Every day
In the Philippines, Cagayan de Oro City
Because we are not together anymore.

My Family
我的家人
Yuqing He

My family is like a ranch,
Happy and noisy.

My dad is a buzzing bee,
Working hard and praying for our good lives.
Sometimes he seems angry to us,
But we know he has good intentions.

My mom is a popular puppy,
She can find many thing we lost.
But sometimes she is lazy and likes talking,
And she loves spending time with her friends.

My younger brother is a prideful pig,
Lazy, only wants to play video games
Eat all my snacks whether sweet or savory
And doesn't wash his face morning and night.

My family is like a ranch.
虽然我的家人有的时候争吵，但是我们依然生活在一起。
(My family sometimes quarrels,
but we are lively and altogether.)

My Family Is Like A Garden
Gerome Luab

My Family is like the backyard
of my house in Landayan

Dad is a mango tree
A lot of *manga* (fruits)
He always gives sweet hugs to me

Mom is a sunflower
Nag pabango (smells like perfume)
The only one who gives me light

Sister is a rose
Rosa like the rose my mom loves
She is *ganda* (beautiful)
Giving smiles to everyone

My Family is like the backyard
of my house in Landayan
with different kinds of happiness

My Family is like the Solar System
Gian Carlo Dupitas

My family is like the Solar System.

My dad is Sun
Strong and providing the needs of our family.

My mom is Earth
Always loving, caring, and giving her all.

My oldest brother is Pluto
Distant but approachable and willing
To listen to my secrets and stories.

My second oldest brother is Saturn
Loves to wear accessories such as rings, earrings, and bracelets
But always missing to shoot the basketball in the ring.

I am Neptune
Always feel cold, but warm inside.
Cracking funny jokes to make my friends happy.

My family is like the Solar System
It's beautiful, living harmoniously
Spreading love and joy far and near.

Roaring Lions
Yong Sheng He

From morning to night, family fights
Like lions roaring at each other

But whenever we do something wrong
We always have each other's backs
No matter what we do
we always stand side by side
As a breeze brings us forward

So we always get along
And wait until dawn
To have another happy day of our life

We have a lot grateful memories through the years
Full of joy, full of tears

The Animal Zoo
John Mathew

My family is like a zoo
We are loud and happy

My father is like a gorilla
He is strong and works hard
He teaches me to climb the tree
And he protects me from enemies

My mom is like a monkey
She's always dancing in the kitchen
Talking to us in ear splitting voice
And she is helpful
She help me with my homework

My younger brother is like a crocodile
He eats all the food on the table
And I am upset

My youngest brother is like an ant
He always bites me
And he's busy with his cellphone

Me and my Cousin are like dogs
We always stick together
And we are always hungry

My family is like a zoo
It can be crazy and noisy but we love each other

♦ ♦ ♦

HEALING

Poetry by the Youth of Kalihi

Almost A Sister
Gentlynn Baelo

She left in 2018
Her tears dropped slowly
My body shook with nerves
You're my best friend
A sister to me.

I remember her smile
Like the sun rising up.
I remember her laugh
When I tell a thousand jokes.
I remember her footsteps
Tapping down the stairs.
Your just a perfect friend
A sister to me.

Now we're a thousand miles apart
With rain drops surrounding me
I always want you by my side
Forever and always
A sister to me.

Before You Judge
Liem Nguyen

Just because I am Vietnamese
Doesn't mean I do not speak English
Doesn't mean I have nothing
Doesn't mean I do not work hard
I am a reliable person.

Just because I am a gamer
Doesn't mean I am an average student
Doesn't mean I am not making money
Doesn't mean I don't help everyone
I always get As in classes and I am very active.

Just because I am poor
Doesn't mean I am not buying something expensive
Doesn't mean I am not smart
Doesn't mean I cannot become the boss of a company someday
I never give up and I can make money.

Just because I am not perfect
Doesn't mean I am lazy
Doesn't mean I am careless
Like imitators who always steal other people's ideas
Doesn't mean I am not intelligent

I am a human and I always try
To learn from my mistakes.

Daughter To Mother
Norina Joseph

Well, mom, I'll tell you
Life for me is a broken earphone
Only one side plays music

That makes me emotional
but relaxed, listening to songs

Even though you're gone
I know you are still with me
Reminiscing about precious time we had
And it still keeps me happy and strong

Memories and music make me want to go back
To when my life was not
A broken earphone.

I am not useless

Mark Sander Alvarez

I can draw with a pencil
That can turn a blank canvas to a masterpiece

I can write poetry with a line
That can forever change someone's mind

I am a good friend
Like how a lion strengthens his cubs

I am not useless
This is how I am
Though, I'm a beautiful being
I am imperfect
That is what I am
And I'm grateful for it.

Lottery and Life
Lance Yuri Quirol

Well I'll tell you a secret.
For me life is like a lottery
Very random
And full of gambling.
And sometimes the odds are against me,

But all the time
I've been playing
And drawing tickets.
Even if I know there's only
a small probability.

So friends, don't give up your ticket
Keep going until the lucky dip
For I still keep betting
Because life is a lottery.

My Guardian

Kane Halle Macadangdang

Life for me has been like a grateful sunflower
As I bloomed for the first time
I heard buzzing around me.
I looked around, but was blinded by the sun.
So I hung my head down

I looked back again, then saw butterflies.
I couldn't explain how happy I was
watching them chasing one another around me.
But they didn't last long as they seperated from one another.
I closed my eyes as the sky became gloomy,
the clouds covered the sun, then rain drops.

Days and weeks passed, until I grew taller and bloomed more.
I've been seeing this beautiful bee everyday.
I realize that she has been guiding me all this time ever since.
Opening my eyes for the second time, 'til I become this flower.
"Would I have bloomed as a sunflower without her guidance?"
I'd say no cuz she been there, watching me grow.
She's been the reason I became more mature.

So lola, I will tell you,
I've been so grateful to have you.
Cuz you were the bee of my life.

Nanang Who
Aisha Mae Bucao

The text was my ticking bomb clicking
Quick tears streamed down for you

For you, who picked me up with wrinkly
old skinny arms that made me laugh
that I purposely jiggled so you could laugh, too

For you, who made me fine toasted sugary bread and honey
who joked impolitely to make me happy whenever I'm gloomy
who walked me to school every day
who I had to help walk across the house

For you, who sometimes told me "Haan ka pay mangan, annako
ngamin nag lukmeg kan," and I responded "Wen, nanang"
but I still ate because food is life. For you, who let me sleep

between Tatang and you, to whom I said "I love you, Nanang Violet.
I'll see you next year ah, and be careful" and who responded
"Aysus, appo ubbing umay–kayon ah."

But the next day, the text
makes my heard drop
strikes the heart of every loved one

"She tripped and hit her head on the ground"

No Longer Here / *KOSE CHIWEN NOMW*
Tarlyn Theodore

You are no longer here,
Yet you chose to appear.

Is it cus I miss you?
Is it cus you miss me?

I can feel the coldness of
your body
Like when you were lying
peacefully.

Am I dreaming?
Is my brain leaking?

Fingers attached to its palm
Are falling.

You are gone,
You are no longer here in this
world,

Yet dad, I can feel you
You are here,

But I chose to be thick-
skinned to your touch
Because it's not true.

Kose chiwen nomw ikei,
Nge ke finata omw kopwe pwá.

Seni ai uwa kon pwositiuk?
Ika ke fen pwositi ei?

Ngang mi mefi patapaten inisum
Usun omw ewe ka senetà non
kinamwe.

Epwe ú tan iká?
A nich tupwuwei?

Éutun pei kei mi pacheri
kumuchui Ra tuttunutiw.

Kose chiwen nomw,
Kose chiwen nomw won ei
fenufan,

Nge papa, ngang mi mefuk
En mi nomw.

Nge uwa pwusin finatá an epwe
kkúm únúchei ngeni ai ei
memmef
Pwun esapw ennetin.

ILY

ILY

45

Queen and Her Knight

Christine Kaye Galutira

Well, mom, I'll tell you:
Life for me is a game of chess
It has checkmates,
wins,
losses,
It's also fun at times
But
All the time the game has been wild
And It's been hard
And It's hectic.

Where are you, Queen?
Your Knight needs you,
So loud and proud, don't you love me?
Don't you care?
'cause you are busy in life
It's like you're not even there.

Don't you know you have a knight?
For if you just want another King
It's an opportunity, and I'll take it,
Because life for me is like a game of chess.

Self to Angelo
Angelo Bermejo

Well, Angelo, I'll tell you, life for me is really empty. Empty like a bottle in the trash. It's really hard to choose alone or happy. My family has their own life, even tho they are boring for me. I make new friends for myself to be happy again. So, Angelo, you can be anything you want to be, go have fun then, be happy, okay, Angelo, don't you fail your life, make it better, for yourself, make your dream come true, make it real for you. But for now. Just. Think. First.

The Same Old Me
Mercy G. Dacoco

Just because I am a teenager
    Doesn't mean I am stupid
    Doesn't mean I live for drama
    Doesn't mean I am always moody
    I am a caring person
    I am always helping my parents.

Just because I am single
    Doesn't mean I am desperate
    Doesn't mean I am a snob
    Doesn't mean I am not attractive
    I am beautiful inside.
    I am fresh every day

Just because I am Filipino
    Doesn't mean I am stubborn
    Doesn't mean I am lazy
    Doesn't mean I am disrespectful
    I am kind
    I always do all my chores

The Sea

Clarisse Agcaoili

Well Mom, i'll tell you
Life for me is the Sea
gigantic and rough waves
Spiky shells and birds flying beyond the sky
It is too deep and you don't know where it ends

But all the time
I've been diving deep down
facing my fears
seeing myself drown
trying to swim back to the shore
Where i feel lost and hopeless.
So Mom, don't you feel sorry
for the times you're not there for me
'cause you always guide me when i struggle

Don't you say you're not there for me when i need your help
For I've been feeling that you're always looking out for me
I am stronger while having you by my side
because life for me is the Sea

To Myself

Eumira Fiesta

She cried with happiness,
With all her heart she's excited
She left with her eyes open
Her soul–it was rising

And as she walks by today
She smiles, she laughs but
Behind it was pain and sadness
She screams through the dark,

And smiles through the broken mirror
And says, tell her it's gonna be okay
Tell her it will end soon
Tell her to endure it
Tell her it'll be worth to wait
I'm standing behind her.

All I can say is bring her down whenever you want
But watch her get up like a rising sun,
With all her confidence you'll believe that
Impossible can be possible.

And thank you for letting her grow this way,
I learned that she will never be the same.

Unmasked
Chanell Kayla Medrano

We people have masks on our face
We are embarrassed to show ourselves
We smile and laugh
The true question is are we really happy?
Is our laugh real?

We try to unmask ourselves in public but we cannot
We only unmask ourselves once we are alone and home

Every time we are masked
We hide the pain so people wouldn't notice
We think that nobody is there for us
To the point we just keep it to ourselves
Even though it's painful we hide it

But people, we need to unmask ourselves
Because there is someone who is there for us
We may not see around us
But we can feel it through our heart
So if we wearing a mask, we need to unmask them now

♦ ♦ ♦

HOME

Poetry by the Youth of Kalihi

About Me

Kevin Cobrador

Me and my friends
Always cutting classes,
In town of Binalbagan.
I was tired at school
Many projects to be done.

Me and my cousins
Harvesting rice,
In my uncle's vast rice field.
And my uncle paid me after work,
The money to help my mother
How happy I was with her bright smiles.

Me and my friends
Playing games,
In a computer shop.
The computer shop called Tito's computer shop
Bang bang I heard gun sounds and
my friend shouting for winning.

Me and my cousins
Struggling with the heavy rice sack,
Under the bright sun
In town of Nabali-an.
Wishing to finish early, go home, and have some rest.

Fefen My Home
Raiercy Francis

I am from the beach
shoreline, bright and breezy,
From a big family
and sparkly gold teeth
From Dolores
and Jann
I'm from telling stories
From be respectful
and be careful

Family weddings and
birthdays
The boom boom band,
Tahitian dancers.
Family funerals
People wailing
and whispering.

Red watermelon,
refreshing cucumber
Sweet potatoes,
pounded breadfruit
Only in Pisinuk, Fefen
my home I like to be.

Ngang seni arosset,
saramaram me enienèochùn
ásápwáán.
Seni ew watten famini
me kimpa mi máretittin
Seni Dolores me J-Ann
Ngang seni tüttùnnap
me kukkunou
Seni manaweni sùfèn
me pwan tumwunèoch

Opwupwunù me upwutiw,
Ewe boom boom band,
pworùkùn Tahiti
Somá non famini
Nguresiresin kechiw me
osokùkkùnùn kapas áán
aramas.

Paren senia,
ammètùn kùùri
Ngaren poteto,
kon mi pwo
Non Pisinuk, neniei
Fefen uwa mochen nömw ie.

(I want it to be the same)
DA Ruben

I am from ocean, blue and wavy
Ngang seni ewe mwataw mi arawarau pwan nónó

From brown skin and different faces
Seni énu-kung me sókopatan maas

From TM and Jemma
Seni TM me Jemma

I'm from the Sunday dinner and watch tv together
Ngang seni mongén nefááf non Ráninifen mé katon fengen tv

I'm from Simmi on Tonowas
Ngang seni Simmi non Tonowas

Sweet banana in coconut milk and fish sashimi
Mwatúnún uuch mi ngarangar me iik mi sasimi

From the time my mom gave birth to my little sister
Seni ewe atun ineiwe aa néunatiw fefineiwe kúkún

Feeling happy like new year's day
Pwapwan netipei usun apwapwan iier mi fé

On my Grandpa's island, the dancing coconut trees
Won fénuwen semei we chinap,ekewe núú rekan pwérukuruk

A welcome gift for our guest
Ew nifangen etiwetiwen noum waséna.

Lovely
Kuhana Osi

I'm from Plumerias, lovely and alive
From many cousins and curly blonde hair
From Oster and Nainai
I'm from family meetings
From be respectful and don't hang out
with the wrong people

I'm from Weno Penia, Mechitiw – –
Delicious, spicy fish and sweet breadfruit
From the sadness of my beloved aunty's memorial service
The sad like crazy, tears like raindrops.

Ngang seni Sèùr, ningèoch pwan manaúanaú
Seni chómmóng tettenin pwii, tettenin mongeei me
mékur mi rùrù pwan parapar
Seni Oster me Nainai
Ngang seni achuffengenni famini
Seni kopwe sufén
Kosapw chiechi ngeni aramas mi ngaw

Ngang seni Weno –Penia, Mechitiw – –
Iik mi anné, fisimwiik, pwan tipen mi ngarangar
Seni ewe fansoun weires ren achechemen söpwonön tettenin ineiwe
Ewe riáffou a ussun upwe fan umwes
Chénun mesei a ussun súrún chénun en ráán.

Love / Yokwe

Aliyah Milne

Love is a potion
I drink without knowing
Love casts a spell
Turns me into a good Samaritan
And drowns me in its deep blue sea
Love takes more energy to control than to let go

Mesmerized by a love so true
Fresh and sweet as the morning dew
Love your neighbor and people around you
Trust in God with all your heart
Remember God's love for you
In every way he will show you
The right direction.

Remember to always

Iakwe ro riturum
Kwõn leke Iroij kõn aolepen būruõṃ
Kwõn jab kõjatdrikrik eok kõn menko kwõj lõmṇak bwe kwõjeḷā
Kwõn kemejmej iroij ilo aolep men ko kwoj kõṃani
Im enaj kwaḷok ñan eok iaḷ eo ejiṃwe
Kwõn jab lõmṇak bwe kwo mālõtlõt ak kwõn kautiej Iroij
Kõṃan eman ñan riturum jab ukõt nana ñan nana
Kõnke iakwe an Iroij ejab bõjrak
iṃ an jouj im tūriamo ejjamin jemḷok.

58

Mountain Boy
Donber Berdon

I am from a mountain, far away and beautiful,
From great singers and hard workers.
From Bereda and Rivian
I'm from praying and big meals
From stay humble and don't go anywhere

Ngang átin won ew chuuk, mi towaw me ningèoch
Seni ew faminien chon kèèn mei pwan achocho lon angang.
Seni Bereda me Rivian
Ngang seni achocho iotek me mongo mi chommong
Seni tipetekison me "Kosapw noo fetan"

I'm from Weno–Neopwa me Epinup,
Juicy red watermelon and sweet breadfruit.
From the month of crying when my grandma died,
The tears like rain
With my mom, my passport to go back to Chuuk,
To plant flowers and vegetables on my mountain.

Ngang seni Weno-Neopwá me Epinupw,
Paren senia mi chènúchèn me ngaren mai
Seni ewe fansoun kechiw ren inei we chinnap a maa seni ei
Surun chènún mesei a ussun pungun en ran
Ren inei we, nei we passport ai upwe niwin ngeni Chuuk,
Ai upwe fföt ira me atake won chukui we.

My Home
Renyrose Esa

I am from a small family
From praying and
going to church
From be respectful and
be humble
From working together and
doing house chores.

I am from the wide ocean,
deep and blue
From women wearing skirts
of green, red, and blue
From cooking big meals and
cleaning the house
From sour pounded
breadfruit and yummy fish

I am from Mama and Papa

I am from Chuuk,
a beautiful necklace,
green island.

Ngang seni ewe kukun family
Seni iotek me
pwan no fan
Seni sufon me
tipetekison
Seni aninnis fengen
pwan fori angangen non imw.

Ngang seni ewe waten sat men
anonon pwan arawaraw
Seni fefin rekan aea uros men
onuwen fetin, par, araw
Seni amwonna waten mongo me
nimeti non imw
Seni kon men mwoon
me ammotun iik

Ngang seni Mama me Papa

Ngang seni Chuuk State, Ekkewe
kukkun fonu ussun epa mwaramwar
mei ningeoch.

My Heart

Marisa Graham

I am from mountains, high and solid.
From obedience and generosity.
From Mama and Papa
I'm from a helping family
From be good
And listen to advice.
I'm from Chuuk, the well-pounded breadfruit and delicious fish.
From the Minister, a loving father.
The jewelry box in my room, saving memories.

Ai Ngasangas

Ngang seni wön chuuk, men tekia me pèchèkkùn
Seni rongosich me kirekireoch
Seni Mama me Papa
Seni ew famini mi aninnisèoch
Seni kopwe aramaséoch
Kopwe rongorong ngeni éùrèùr.
Ngang seni Chuuk, ùsùèochchùn kon me ammétùn iik.
Seni ewe Soukoa, semei mi uren tong.
Ewe pwörun pisek mi auchea non rumweiwe, nenien pisekin
achechem.

My Motorcycle and My Life
Alex Junior Raza

In a far away town called Dingras
a place I love that I call home
Made of kawayan and pan-aw was built.
We were contented with what we had
Because love was always there
My parents provided for our needs
Like a motorcycle full of bliss

But luck sometimes is not for me
Because bad luck is hunting me

My close friend and I went cruising on a hot
Summer day, we stopped by a blue green river
A quick dive, fun and happy day
Turned into a sad and aching one.
As we drove back home
Excited and tired from swimming
We suddenly hit a big rock on the dusty road
We were thrown on the ground and fell-flat on our faces

When I woke up it wasn't a good dream, it was real.
I had a motorcycle accident.

My Sisters and I
Cheska Rivera

My sisters and I
Travel to Taiwan for vacation
Walk in the streets
Listen to some love songs
Buy some wallets for my aunties in the Philippines
Smell new fruity perfume

My sisters and I
In my house made of bricks in Baguio City
Small kitchen with a rectangular table for four girls
Wash the pots and pans
Scrub the shiny floor
Cook our favorite noodles, sam yang
Eat vegetables together always made us happy

My sisters and I
Swim in the cold pool
Talk about our friends and cousins
Play billiards
Walk in the park in Burnham
Ride on a boat in San Juan Bay
Drink milk tea
Call me Bek Bek

I miss those days

Ramson to Poseidon
Ramson Tedor

Well, Poseidon, I'll tell you
Life for me is the sea.

It has colorful fishes that look like the rainbow
And mermaids and clam shells
that have my name painted on it.
But sometimes
I've seen sharks devouring fishes
And the shark scares away the mermaids.

But don't be agitated because of sharks
I have a spear for the shark's tail

Fishes and mermaids thank me for saving them
Mermaids take me of out the water.
The water sweeps over my feet
Where I stand the waves whisper to me
Calling me to go to the soft sand.
A mermaid points up to the land

When I look at the mountain it stands very tall
That is why life for me is the sea
Despite obstacles and difficulties,
it has pleasant things in it.

Poseidon I will see you in the deep blue.

POETS

Youth of Kalihi

Clarisse Jane Agcaoili

I grew up in Vintar, Ilocos Norte, Philippines, but my parents moved our family from Philippines to Hawai'i in 2013. Now that I live in Honolulu, I still speak Ilokano and Tagalog at home. This project surprised me because I didn't know that I can use Ilokano words in my projects. I want to be famous one day so that people will listen to my voice. This poetry anthology is just the beginning of my journey.

Tuieteuati Eugene Alai

I was born and raised in American Samoa. I moved to the State of Hawai'i in 2018. I speak the language of Samoa. I feel so good and excited because this is the first time I am using my voice by writing as an author. My ultimate dream is to become an actor, which is why my primary goal is to pursue an education. Faafetai tele lava ma manuia tou taumafaiga tupulaga mo le lumana'i. Thank you very much and God bless teens with grit for our future.

Maremingy Alifios

I moved to Hawaiʻi from Guam in 2018. I grew up in Guam and I went to Chuuk for a few months. When I was in Chuuk, I realized that it is different because it is great to stay there because of the good scenery but people are poor. I don't think I'm good at poetry, but this poetry turned out to be exciting because I'm starting to learn how to do the stanzas, and I also figured that I don't need commas. My mom and my grandma always tell me, "Ajojo pwe kopwe anisi kem," which means, "Work hard so you can help us and get a better future." I want to be a lawyer because it pays well and I will be able to take care of them.

Mark Sander Alvarez

I was born in Laoag City, Ilocos Norte, Philippines, at the northern part of Luzon. I speak Ilokano, Tagalog, and English. This project will help with my writing skills and help me in journalism class. This project will also promote different cultures or ethnicities such as Chuukese, Vietnamese, Chinese, Marshallese, and Samoan culture. My dream is to help those who are suffering or struggling from mental illness and adverse childhood experiences. I also dream of improving my artistic dexterity. I don't remember the words of wisdom from my country, so I created my own, "Instead of putting stacks of failures on your shoulders, build a staircase out of your mistakes to propel you in life."

Gentlynn Baelo

I was born here in Hawai'i in 2002. I am the only girl in my family. I went to Chuuk in 2015 and when I came back in 2018 I did not really know how to speak English anymore. I just stayed on my island for two years, but it was a long time for me to not speak English, so when I came back my mom told me to not speak Chuukese anymore and to use English at all time. Even though I'm tired of speaking English, I will still not give up coming to school. At the beginning of this project I thought it was hard for me, but I found the aha moment and now I will never give up. This project is fun for me now and not boring at all. My mom would always say, "Jenjen kosapw fangetá non ömw na school pun kopwe support ach ei family." So I say when I graduate and finish high school, I am the only one who will support my family and make them proud.

Angelo Bermejo

I am from the Philippines. I was born on May 24, 2004 and I moved to Hawai'i when I was four years old. I live with my mom, my three brothers, and two sisters. I speak English at home. I don't much speak Tagalog because I have been here in Hawai'i for nine years. My poem makes me feel happy because it gives me energy. Now I feel like I can write more interesting books. In the future my goal is to become a better writer. I want to write a book of poems on my own.

Dayson Berdon

I am from Weno in Chuuk. I came to Hawai'i in 2017. I can speak Chuukese. Writing this poem made me feel nervous because it's the first time that I'm going to write a book. I am excited for people to read my poem because I want to share my story. My family always says, "kopwe mwösönösön." This means be humble so people will be nice to you. I do this every single day. My dream is to join the U.S. Navy.

Donber Berdon

I am from Nantaku Neopwe in Chuuk. I came to Hawaiʻi in 2017. I can speak Chuukese language. Writing this poem made me feel proud of myself because I think I did a good job on my project. My family always says "Kosapw nöfetán." This means, "Donber don't go anywhere." They say this to protect me. My dream is to travel to Portland, Oregon because I want to go visit my brother and my auntie.

Aisha Mae Bucao

I was born in the Philippines, I moved to Hawai'i in 2010. Honestly, I can only speak English. I can speak just a little bit of Ilokano but I can understand it clearly. I think this project is a great way to express our feelings. It is like using our voice as a "weapon" to heal from the situation we are in. My only goal for the future is to just live my life peacefully, I hope. "Agsingsingpetka, anakko" is what my grandparents always tell me.

Eddie Casallo

I grew up in the Philippines in the town of Nagbukel in Ilocos Sur prior to moving to Hawai'i. I can still speak my Ilokano but I'm using English so people can understand me. This project surprised me because it allows me to write about my feelings and my childhood. I would like to be famous one day so my voice can be heard.

Anisa Chikuo

I am from Polle Neirenom in Chuuk. I came to Hawaiʻi on July 14, 2016. I can speak Chuukese. Writing this poem made me feel scared because this is the first time I did a project like this. Now I feel excited because I know how to write a poem. My family always says, "Kopwe pwáár ngeni aramas omw sùfèn." This means always be respectful. My dream is to go back to Chuuk to be with my friends and family.

Wojila Chutaro

I am from the Marshall Islands and I am fifteen years old. My favorite food is energy food that gives me a healthy life. I would like to travel all around the world so I can learn new things from others. I speak English and Marshallese. I remember when I first came to Hawai'i last year, I missed my family back home, but I love Hawai'i now because there are a lot of delicious foods and movie theaters. I feel excited about being in this project because this is my first time writing poems and publishing it. So, I'm going to be famous after all. Also, my dream is to become a famous nurse. I remember my grandfather always telling me "kwõn kõrã im an kõl luweo einwot kar libubu eo aṃ," which means be grateful and strong like your grandma.

Christian Cobrador

I was born in the Himamaylan province of Negros Occidental, Philippines. I moved to Hawai'i in 2018. I can speak Ilonggo, Tagalog, English, and a little bit of Ilokano. I feel nervous and excited since this is my first time writing poetry. I'm still not sure of my dreams for the future, but I want to graduate from college.

Kevin Cobrador

I'm from the Philippines and I'm fourteen years old. I came to Hawai'i in 2018 because my aunty wanted my siblings and I to finish school and have a good job. My first language is Ilonggo. I speak this language with my friends. I only speak English in school. My cousins are important in my life. They are poor in the Philippines and attending college without enough money to buy things for school so they ask my father to lend some money. That is why my father always tells me, "swerti gid kay naka kadto kamo sa Hawai'i" (you're so lucky because you came to Hawai'i). I don't want to waste this opportunity in Hawai'i, so I will study hard. When I finally finish college, I will have a good job. Then, I will help my family and relatives in the Philippines.

James Zyrus Comision

I'm 14 years old and I'm from the Philippines. I was born in Cagayan de Oro City in my auntie's house. I speak Visayan, Ilonggo, Tagalog, and English. My dream is to finish this school high school year and to attend college. I came to Hawai'i on March 13, 2018. When I moved here to Hawai'i, my heart was broken in a million pieces. I couldn't believe that I had to leave my friends and classmates in the Philippines. It hurt me a lot and made me cry, but made my parents want me to have a great future, so I had to accept it. I miss my friends a lot, but I have made my friends here to help me get over it. I feel happy to do this project because I will be an author of a book. My dream is get a good job like joining the Navy.

Mercy G. Dacoco

I am Filipino. I was born in Ilocos Norte. I came here in Hawaiʻi on January 17, 2019. I speak Ilokano and Tagalog, and now I'm learning how to speak English. When I came to Hawaiʻi, I remember I went to Ala Moana Mall. I enjoyed shopping at the beautiful stores. I also remember when we drove around the island, I saw beautiful beaches. I felt very happy to be in Hawaiʻi because I finally saw the beauty of Hawaiʻi. My mom always tells me, "agan-annadka, anakko" (be careful). My goal for the future is to become a nurse because I want to help people who are sick and I want to take care of my parents when they get sick. I realize that, to reach my goals and dreams, I need to concentrate and work hard as a student.

John John Daluping

I am 16 years old. I am from the Philippines. I speak Tagalog, Ilokano, and English. I first came to Hawaiʻi in November 2018 and I felt happy because I found my crush when I was playing basketball. I feel happy about being in this project because I am learning how to write English poems. My dream is to finish college and to become a fireman. My parents always tell me, "mag aral kang mabuti" (study hard). That is why I'm striving hard to study, so I could achieve my goals in life and help my family.

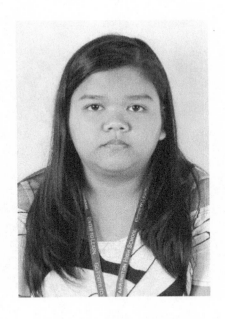

Jonalyn Daluping

I am 14 years old. I am from Ilocos Sur Philippines. I speak Tagalog, Ilokano, and English. I came to Hawai'i four months ago. I feel happy about being in this project because I am sharing about my life, future, and my language. I want to become a flight attendant because I want to help my family financially and want my family to be proud of me. My oldest brother always tells me, "huwag munang maki boyfriend unahin muna ang pag aaral" (study first before having a boyfriend). That is why I am trying my best to be a good daughter, sister, and student in school.

Gian Carlo R. Dupitas

I am 16 years old. I am from the Philippines and now I live in Hawai'i. I speak Ilokano and Tagalog. And sometimes, if they don't understand my language, I try to speak English, so that they can understand me. I came to Hawai'i in February, 2018. When I first came to Hawai'i, I remember my family and I hiked in Koko Crater. I was so tired because the mountain was so high and steep, but when we were done, the view was so spectacular. I could see so many mountains and beautiful beaches. When I heard about the poetry project, I was afraid because I thought that it would be hard. But now, I feel great because it is fun to write poems. My dream is to join the military and form a happy family. That is my goal.

Charleen Eram

I am from Tol Faichuuk in Chuuk. I came to Hawaiʻi on March 30, 2017. I can speak English a little bit. Writing this poem made me feel happy about this project because this is my first time writing poetry. My family always says, "Sùfèn." This means to be respectful. I think about this every day. My dream is to become a doctor in Chuuk because I want to help people on my island.

Renyrose Esa

I am from Wolip in Chuuk. I came to Hawaiʻi on April 17, 2018. I can speak Chuukese and English. This project made me feel happy because I like the poem I wrote. I liked being able to talk about me and my family. But I am still scared to read my poem in front of people. My family always says, "kopwe achocho sikun." This means, "work hard in school." They tell me this because they want me to learn English. After high school, I want to have a job working at the airport so it is easy to go back to Chuuk.

Jalen Jor Espejo

I moved to Hawaiʻi from the Philippines on March 2, 2018. I grew up in Pagudpud, Ilocos Norte, where I enjoyed swimming and playing in the pure white sands of its beaches. I can speak and understand both Tagalog and Ilokano, although I use Ilokano more often than Tagalog. I always enjoyed writing poems. It's one of the ways I express my thoughts rather than talking to others. I have always been the private type, saying I'm okay even though I'm not. I don't like letting people know what I feel or making them worry, so I keep it in and write about what I really feel.

Wersi Farata

I grew up in Kalihi, but my parents are still back in Chuuk. I was born in Chuuk, but my grandma and aunties raised me here in Honolulu. I can somewhat speak Chuukese, but I don't really use that language because sometimes I pronounce words wrongly. My grandma and aunties always tell me to focus in school, no boyfriends yet. Finish school then you can have all the fun you want. Because of them, I want to be a teacher or a nurse one day.

Eumira Fiesta

I grew up in San Nicolas, Ilocos Norte, Philippines. I moved to Hawaiʻi in November, 2017. I am a full-blooded Filipino and can understand Tagalog, Ilokano, and English. In addition, I'm looking forward to learning Korean. This project is important to me because it will help me publish my own book in the future. I really enjoy expressing my feelings through writing poems, composing music, and drawing. But, I'm most confident in using my voice by writing poems.

Raiercy Francis

I am from Ochoch Kurry Fefen in Chuuk. I came to Hawai'i in 2017. I can speak Chuukese and English. Writing this poem made me feel surprised because I didn't think I was able to do this. My family always says, "kopwe achocho nön sukun." This means, "Work hard in school." They tell me this because they want me to finish school and go to college. My dream is to be a hard working person in order to help my family.

Mark Jayson Atendido Fuerte

I was born in Vigan, Philippines. I came to Hawaiʻi in September 2013. The languages I speak are Ilokano, Tagalog, English, and little bit of Spanish. I feel lucky to be a part of this project because this is the first time my writing will be included in a published book. My dream in the future is to be a pilot or a basketball player.

Christine Kaye Galutira

I was born in Ilocos Norte, Philippines. I speak Ilokano, Tagalog, and English. I moved to Hawai'i in 2016. This project was a good opportunity for me to explain my thoughts through poetry. Now, I know I can use my voice by writing my feelings. I feel honored to be published in a book.

Marisa Graham

I am from Wonuset in Chuuk. I came to Hawai'i in 2018. I can speak Chuukese. Writing my poem made me feel excited because it is my first time ever writing one and I can tell my story. My family always says, "Kosapw namanam tekia." This means to always be humble. My dream is to go to college.

Yong Sheng He

I came to Hawaiʻi in 2009. I grew up in Guangzhou and moved here when I was six. I can speak Cantonese, Mandarin, and English. This project excites me because it can make me famous and change me!

Yuqing He

I am 15 years old. I speak Mandarin and English. My name in Chinese means "sunny day after a rain." My favorite colors are light blue and magenta. On January 16, 2016, I first came to Hawai'i. My mother says, "你需要多看 和听英语视频," which means, "you need to watch and listen to English videos." When I first started coming to school, I felt scared because didn't know much English. I feel happy about being in this project, because I can express my feelings through poems. My dream is to become a painter.

Norina Joseph

I was born and raised in Kalihi, but my siblings and parents moved from Guam to Oahu in 2002. Even though I was born and raised in Oahu, I still understand the language when my parents speak Chuukese. I feel nervous about this project because I think my poem is not good poetry to others. My goals for the future are to have a good life and never fall for bad things.

Adrian James F. Lo

I grew up in the Philippines. I arrived in Hawai'i on September 16, 2018 so I'm very new to Hawai'i and to its culture. For example, the traffic rules and regulations here are very clean and every driver follows the rules but in my hometown it is way different. I can speak three languages, Bicol, Tagalog, and English. I'm very excited for this book because I'm the kind of person that loves to try new things, especially being a part of this project. Like my parents always tell me in our language, "Walang impossible kung di mo gagawin nang maayos." In English, "there is nothing impossible if I'm not working hard." This has always been an inspiration for me when I'm doing something different and trying something new.

Gerome Luab

I was born in Laguna City. I came to Hawai'i on September 5, 2018. I learned how to speak Bisaya, Tagalog, and English. I feel good about this poetry project because I learned how to speak more English while asking for advice from my teachers and talking to my classmates. My dream is to help my mom when she gets older. My goal is to become a businessman. "Mag aral ka mabuti" (study hard). My mom often says this and I feel happy because it means she always cares for me.

Kane Halle Macadangdang

I was born in the province of Ilocos Norte, and I moved to Hawai'i in 2016. I can understand and speak my home language which is Ilokano. I'm not that good at writing poems, so this project is new to me. Someday, I want to be a Registered Nurse so I can help other people especially my loved ones.

Chanell Kayla Medrano

I was born in Manila, Philippines but moved to Hawai'i in 2010. I speak Ilokano and Tagalog, but mostly in Tagalog. I really enjoyed this project because of how we can use our voice as a weapon by writing our thoughts or speaking out. We can show people who have been through similar experiences that they are not alone. I want to be a nurse someday so I can help others, especially my family who has health problems. My goals are to have a decent job and have a perfect family. I've been in Hawai'i the last nine years.

Aliyah Milne

I was born and raised in the Marshall Islands and I moved to Hawaiʻi last year in June 2018. I speak Marshallese and a little English. I can understand English, but sometimes it is hard for me to speak, but I try my best. I think this project is good for us because we get to share our thoughts and it helps us understand more. I want to build my own business and ikōṇaan juon eo enaj kōṃṃan jabdrewot ñan baaṃle eo an.

Chan Ai Nguyen

I was born and raised in a small city in Vietnam. In the fall of 2018, my family moved to Hawaiʻi. I speak Vietnamese and English. This project is very new to me, I am very excited and it is an opportunity for me to learn more. My mother always says to me "Suy nghĩ kĩ trước khi quyết định bỏ cuộc,và nghĩ đến lí do con bắt đầu," and that reminds me when I get bored and want to stop something, I should look back on what I tried. My goal is to become a fashion business woman, I want my mother and all women to become more beautiful.

Liem Phuoc Nguyen

I was born and grew up in Ca Mau, South Vietnam. I can speak Vietnamese and English. When I first came to Hawai'i, it was July, 2018. On the day I left, I saw many airplanes and I felt excited because it was the first time I was on an airplane. Then, I went to a Vietnamese restaurant because I already felt homesick. But when I came to school, I felt great because I could hear everyone speaking English and other languages. I feel great joining this project because it makes me feel that I can talk about what is going on in my mind. My dream is to become a billionaire. I want to help my big family come to U.S. by staring my own company or joining the military. When I get older, I want to open a coffee shop. "Hãy luôn tôn trọng người khác," which means show respect to everyone. This sentence is what old Vietnamese people usually say to their grandchildren to teach us our values.

Kuhana Osi

I am from Weno, Chuuk. I came to Hawaiʻi in 2017. I can speak Chuukese. Writing this poem made me feel proud because I feel empowered about my culture. My family always says "achocho nön ömw sikun." This means work hard and study hard in school. My dream is to join the Olympic games for track and field and represent Chuuk State.

Ariel Jhames Battad Peralta

Please call me AJ. I was born in Calamagui Provincial Hospital. I came to Hawai'i on August 3, 2018. I speak Tagalog, Ilokano, and English. You can talk to me with any language you want. I feel happy about this poetry project because it's fun, although it is a little bit difficult. My dream is to help other people, join the Air Force, and help my mom because I want to take care of my family. My uncle, aunt, mom, and dad say to me all the time, "mag aral kang mabuti" (study hard). I must work hard in school. I feel inspired to become a better person.

Lance Yuri Quirol

I grew up in the Philippines, but my whole family moved to Hawai'i in 2017. I can speak two languages, which are Tagalog and English. One example of a Tagalog phrase my parents always say to me is "mag-ingat ka" which means be safe. For me, this project was very difficult because I am shy and not confident in my work. Showing my poem to other people was challenging but I still tried because I thought it would be a great learning experience.

John Mathew Raras

I am from Laoac, Pangasinan, Philippines. I'm 17 years old and I speak different languages like Tagalog, Ilokano, and English. I first came here in Hawaiʻi in August 2018. I feel happy about being in this project because I like to write poems and I want to be better at writing poetry. My dream is to become a successful businessman someday. My parents always tell me "aggagetka anakko tapno rumang-ay ti biagmo" (be diligent to have a successful life). That is why I'm striving hard to study so I can reach my goal in my life.

Alex Jr. R. Raza

I'm 15 years old. I'm from the province of Ilocos Norte in the Philippines and now I live in Hawaiʻi. I speak Ilokano at home and speak Tagalog and English at school. When I first came to Hawaiʻi in 2017, I remember being sad about my family members I left behind in the Philippines. I feel happy about being in this project because I learned how to write poems. My goal is to finish college. I want to join the US Air Force and have a happy family. Before my grandma passed away she always told me "agsingsingpetka ken agadalkayo a nasayaat" (be good and study hard). That's why I'm trying my best to be a good son and student, so my parents and grandparents will be proud of me.

Cheska Rivera

I was born in Baguio City and moved to San Fernando when I was 9. I speak Tagalog and English. I use English in school, and at home, I speak Tagalog. My nickname is Bek-Bek. I am the youngest of three siblings. When I first came to Hawai'i this year, I remember how excited and happy I was. I heard a lot of good things about Hawai'i before I came here. For example, Hawai'i is very beautiful and has many clean beaches. I was not disappointed to see some lovely, calm, and clean beaches here in Hawai'i. Also, I felt happy to see my grandmother and grandfather here. I feel this poetry project is challenging, but I like to try new things. I have never written any poems in the Philippines. In the future, I want to become a physical therapist in Hawai'i. To achieve my dream, I will study hard so that I can help my parents financially and help people who are sick.

Bermackson Ress

I am from Pawnai in Chuuk. I came to Hawai'i in 2014. I can speak English and Chuukese. Writing this poem made me feel good because in my life I like to write down my feelings and I want to share them with other people. I hope that people have same feelings that I have. In my family, my mom always says, "Achocho nön ömw sukun." This means to not give up keep on doing what you believe. This makes me think that my mom really cares about me. My dream is to be a singer or a rapper and to help take care of my mom.

John Dhread Rosete

I was born on April 18, 2004. When I was ten years old, in 2014, my parents and I moved from the Philippines to Oʻahu, Hawaiʻi. My first language is Ilokano and I learned a little bit of English from cartoons. My grandparents always tell me "agsingsingpetka" which means to behave. I feel pretty confident because I wrote a poem about how I actually felt when I was arriving in Hawaiʻi. I don't really feel shy about sharing my poem because I want people to know how I feel. My dream for the future is to become a music producer.

DA Ruben

I came to Hawai'i in 2017. I can speak English and Chuukese. Writing this poem made me feel happy because I get to explain how I feel. My family always says, "kopwe rongosich." This means "Be obedient." They want me to have a good life. My dream is to have a beautiful house so that people can come visit me from Chuuk and have a place to sleep.

Ronilo Alinsugay Santander

I am 16 years old. I was born in Tagum City in Mindanao on May 6, 2002. I speak Bisaya, Tagalog, and English. My home country is so cool because there are lots of vendors selling foods like isaw and fishball and it's only 5 pesos. I came to Hawai'i on December 22, 2018. The first time I came to Hawai'i, I felt sad because I missed my dad and my friends in the Philippines. But, so far, I made new friends here and I feel happy. I feel excited to be in this poetry project because I learned how to write poems. My dream is to graduate from college. I want to become an engineer.

Trinity E. Stephen

I'm from a small island in the Pacific Ocean, which is Chuuk. I know some people have never heard of this small island but it's okay, I'll tell you about it. Chuuk has the most beautiful ocean and nicest beaches. I was born and raised in Chuuk. I came here to Honolulu, Hawaiʻi in 2019 to visit my grandparents on my mom's side. Mostly all of us in my family know how to speak Chuukese and English, but most of the time we speak Chuukese because that's what my family wants for us. They always say we should speak Chuukese because we might forget it. The project I did was not really fun because I have a hard time thinking of what to write or how to write it with good grammar. I'm the type of girl that still has a slow mind. But I'm thankful that I did something. In the future I want to be a person that has a fast mind, like when I have homework I can just look at it and already know how to do it. My goal is to finish school and get a degree to make my family proud.

Ramson Tedor

I was born in Kalihi in 2004, and sometimes I stay in Waianae. I only speak English but I am learning how to speak Chuukese. My dreams and goals in the future are to live a happy and simple life.

Tarlyn Theodore

I am eighteen years old and am from the tiny and beautiful island of Churri Maram located in Chuuk, Micronesia. In 2009, I moved to the city of Honolulu due to the lack of many things back home, but most importantly, education. I grew up in a caring family where traditions and culture are important. I grew up learning what is wrong and what is right and also to not forget our own language, which is Chuukese. I didn't expect that I would do a project for this class, but I am thankful towards Ms. Ellie for giving me this opportunity to express how I feel. I would be honest and say that I'm a person who dreams big. My dreams seem impossible, but I believe that anything is possible if we have God in our lives. I was dreaming, now I'm awake. I am a proud Micronesian and forever will be.

Alodia Ann Villanueva

I'm currently in 9th grade. I speak Ilokano, Tagalog, and English. I was born in the Philippines and I came to Hawai'i last year. I am a funny and loving girl with a good sense of humor. One thing about me that is important for you to know is that, at first, you might think that I am a very shy girl, but once you get to know me, I become friendly and jolly. I feel happy about being in this project because I like challenges and I like doing new things. I am excited to have my poem published. My future goal is to join the US Army and serve my new country. My mom always tells me "agan-anuskayo anakko" (be patient my child). I'm thankful because she guides me daily to do what is right.

Lemin Xu

I came to Hawai'i from China in 2018. I've only been here for half a year, so I can only speak Chinese. I don't think I am good at English poetry because rhyme for me is difficult, I cannot do it well. I want to go back to China and be an accountant. There is a saying in China, "不是你的，　别落你的袋 (Bu shi ni de cai, bie luo ni de dai)." This means, "Not your wealth, don't put it in your bag." Be down to earth, don't be greedy.

Hanting Zhou

I am from China. I came to Hawai'i in 2018. I speak Mandarin. This project is really interesting because I like writing poetry to share my feelings and experiences. I want to be an excellent person in whatever field I go into in the future. There is an old saying in China, "Huo dao lao, xue dao lao." It means you are never too old to learn. I will keep learning anything I do not know.

TEACHERS

Educators of the Youth of Kalihi

Elianna Kantar

I was born and raised in Minneapolis, Minnesota in an English-speaking household where Hebrew and Yiddish phrases peppered most conversations. In 2017, I was given the opportunity to come to Farrington High School and be an ELL teacher so I packed my bags and moved to Hawai'i. As a teacher, my goal has always been to foster an environment where students feel safe, supported, and encouraged to follow their passions. I want my students to not only succeed in school, but also to find the joy in simply learning. At Farrington, I work with a small population of our language learners, many of whom are new to the United States and have had limited or interrupted formal education experiences. I am continuously struck by the kindness, honesty, and curiosity these students walk into my classroom with every single day. This project has allowed me to share my students with others and to showcase these incredible young people that have made Hawai'i their home through a platform that allows them to control and tell their own stories.

Norman Sales

I grew up in Bacarra, Ilocos Norte, Philippines. I speak Ilokano, Tagalog, and English. I am an English teacher and the head of the English Language Arts Department at Farrington High School. I am also a member of Farrington's Teacher Leadership Cadre, a diverse group of teachers who facilitates school wide professional development. I started teaching the sheltered English classes for freshman English Language Learners in 2013. As an immigrant myself, I empathize with my students' challenges in navigating their new home. I seek ways to empower my students in the classroom, at our school, and in our community. I also value my students' unique experiences and home culture so this poetry anthology helps us celebrate their heritage, languages, and histories.

Akiko Giambelluca

Our English Learners (ELs) are storytellers, navigators, farmers, dancers, mathematicians, athletes, artists, and philosophers. They just don't know how to express themselves and people don't know who our ELs are because they are marginalized, underestimated, and often forgotten. I am an EL teacher and also a coordinator supervising the EL program at Farrington High School. I have been teaching at FHS for 12 years and I really enjoy working with EL students from various backgrounds and with different perspectives. Born and raised in Japan, I'm fluent in both Japanese and English. Living in Hawai'i for the past 20 years, I have found Hawai'i to be an ideal place for immigrant students to perpetuate their own cultures, appreciate indigenous culture, and learn about mainstream culture in the U.S. For each of us, our cultural background shapes our identity. Knowing ourselves is the first step in learning about a new culture. Through this project, I hope our students and I will grow and take pride in our own cultures. Also, I hope those who read these poems can understand the struggles and joys of growing up in a new country. Just listen to their voices.

Rachel Chaerin Jun

My name is Rachel Chaerin Jun. I was born and raised in Seoul, South Korea and moved to Hawaiʻi in 2008. Similar to many English language students, I barely knew any English when I first came here. After experiencing the difficulties of learning a new language, I was inspired to pursue a career in language education because I believe I understand students' struggles. In my two semesters at Farrington High School as a student teacher, one of my foci in teaching has been about establishing rapport with my students. Developed positive relationships have encouraged them to talk to me using the target language, opening up further opportunities for improving their English skills. On that continuum, I am honored to be a part of this poetry project. Aside from encouraging students to use the language for mere everyday conversations, this project has taught me how to empower students to use their voices to express themselves about injustice issues they face.

MAHALO

Community Partners and Donors
Farrington Alumni Community Foundation
Farrington High School Administration, Faculty, and Staff
Filipino Association of University Women
Inda and John Gage
Matson Community Giving Foundation
Pacific Resources for Education and Learning
Parent and Children Together

Volunteer Editors
Amalia Bueno
Rose Churma
Stu Glauberman
Leni Knight
Pepi Nieva
Elmer Pizo
Marie Antonette Ramos

Mentors
Dwight Ong
Giovanni Ortega

Book Reviewers
Patricia Halagao
Craig Perez Santos
Catherine Ritti

Book Cover Design
Calvin Bagaoisan

Photographs
Corey "Cuyote" Harkins
Aljon Tacata
Farrington High School Photography

Media Support
Radiant Cordero
Lalaine Ignao

Heritage Language Support
Flodeliz Alob
Dean Antonio Domingo
Almond Jaye Ereno
Zaida Magday
Maybellene Marar
Chelsea Phillip
Erika Rekis
Monica Reimers

Made in the USA
Las Vegas, NV
17 February 2024

85883381R00080